ENTER THE DRAGON
SCRAPBOOK SEQUENCES
VOLUME 3

Enter the Dragon (Chinese:龍爭虎鬥) is a 1973 martial arts film directed by Robert Clouse and written by Michael Allin. The film stars Bruce Lee, John Saxon and Jim Kelly. It was Lee's final completed film appearance before his death on 20th July 1973 at the age of 32. An American and Hong Kong co-production, it premiered in Los Angeles on 19th August 1973, one month after Lee's death. The film is estimated to have grossed over US$400 million worldwide (estimated to be the equivalent of over $2 billion adjusted for inflation as of 2022), against a budget of $850,000. Having earned morethan 400 times its budget, it is one ofthe most profitable films of all time as well as the most successful martial arts film

Welcome to the third volume of "Enter the Dragon" sequences, showing more pictures of one of Asia's most photographed man. By the time Bruce filmed "Enter the Dragon" he would be photographed almost every minute he was on and off set.

We can only be grateful that due to the actions of the cameramen on set, we now have thousands of images capturing his art, his expressions and his emotions

In these volumes, we highlight just a few of the many photos takenduring filming capturing him often in sequences as the camera clicked away.

In the beginning we only flirted with martial art movies, It was not until Bruce Lee came along that we fell in love them

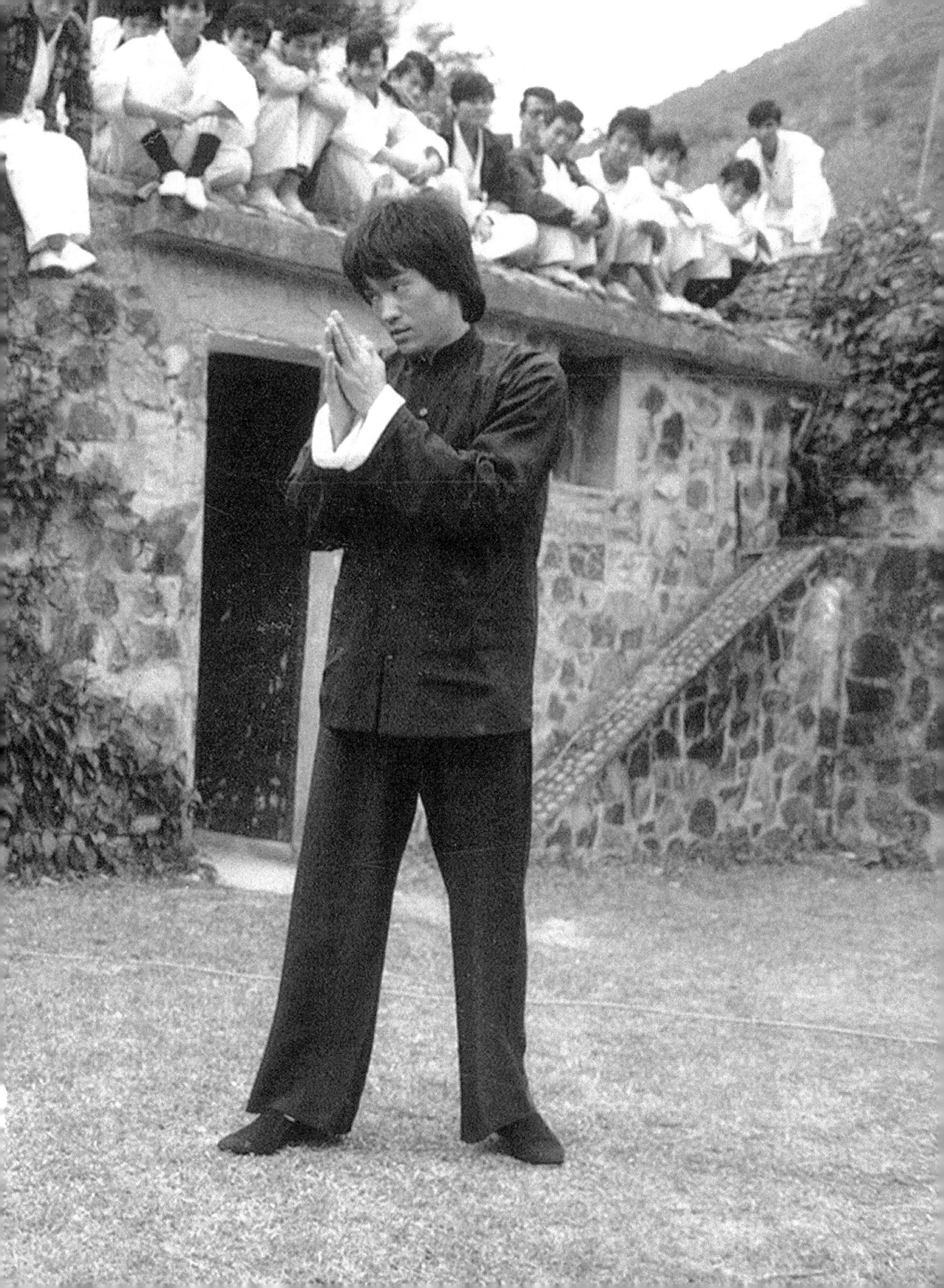

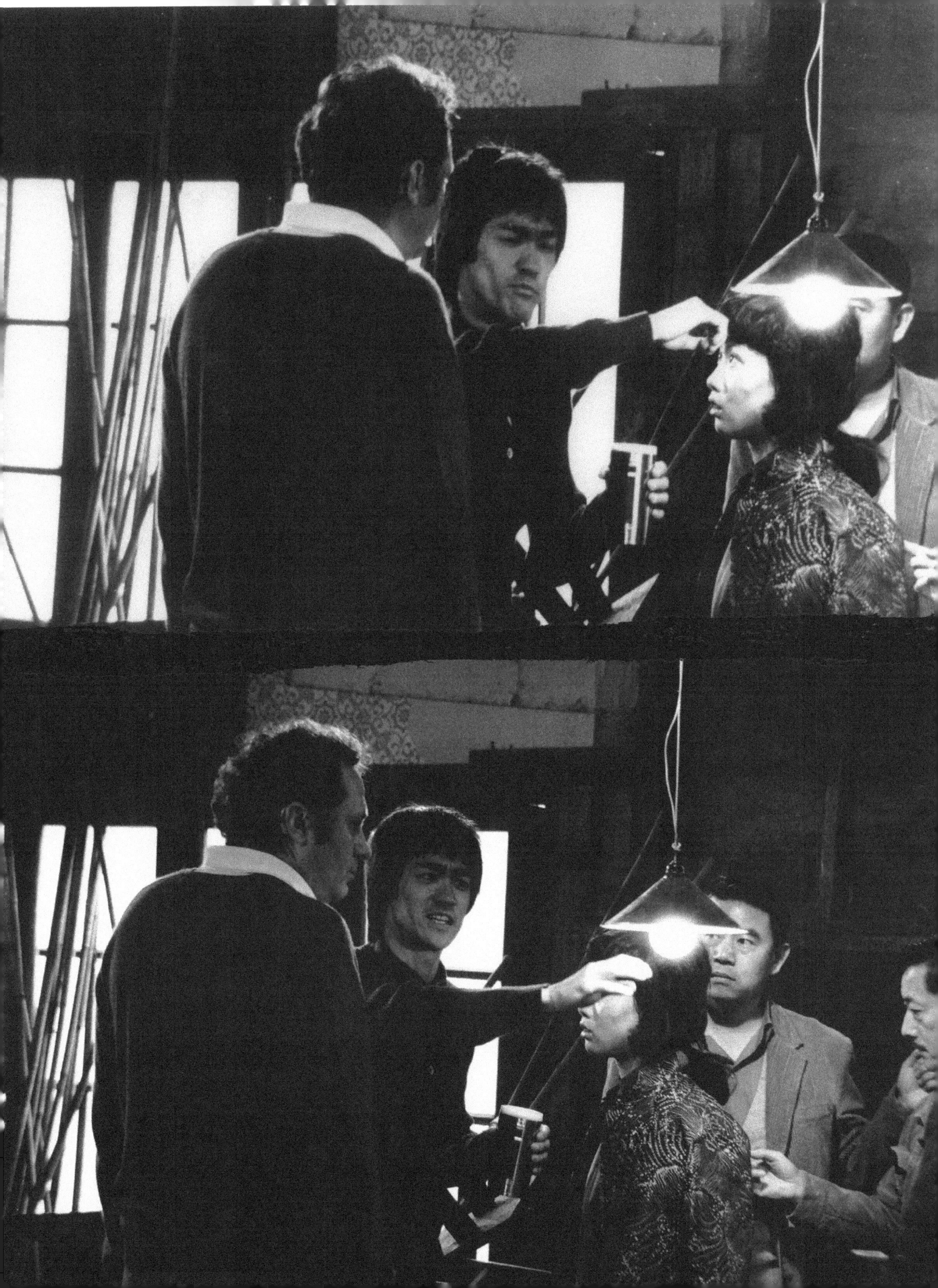

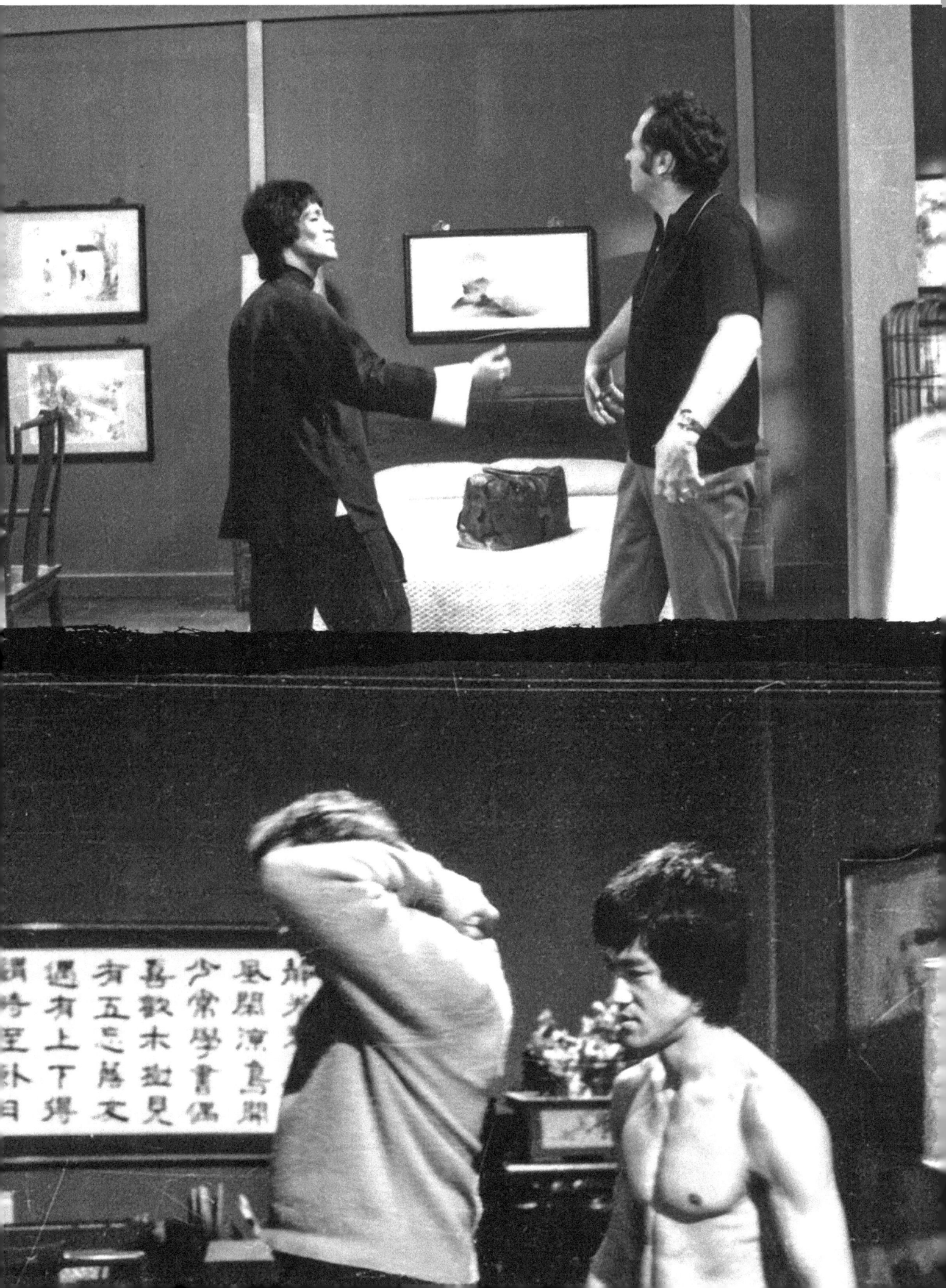

www.ingramcontent.com/pod-product-compliance
Lightning Source LLC
Chambersburg PA
CBHW051317110526
44590CB00031B/4386